May God
Bless you
Never forget it

Daughter of the Most High

7 Days to Pray
the
Single Away

Nakitah Shannon

#DMH

7 Days to Pray the Single Away

Nakilah Shannon

Judah House
Press

Copyright © 2013 by Nakilah Shannon

ISBN 13: 978-0615899923

ISBN 10: 0615899927

Judah House Press
P.O. Box 55472
Indianapolis, Indiana 46205
judahhousepress.com

This book was printed in the United States of America

Contents

Preface

Dear Single Sisters,

This book is dedicated to you. No matter how you got to this season, the reality is you are here. Now my challenge and question to you is this, "what will you do next?" Will you wallow and complain during this time or will you regain your sense of freedom? My desire and purpose of this book is that you will choose to move forward. I want us to stop avoiding the question, "So why are you still single?" Start giving God-pleasing answers. I want us to no longer be afraid to accept our singleness, but to celebrate it while anticipating our coming union. I want us to walk with our heads up high, not ashamed of being single and not ashamed of wanting to be a wife someday. I want us to wait in a way that's pleasing to God and in a way that frees us from society's standards. As "church girls" we're expected to be a certain way when we are single. We're supposed to be single, saved and satisfied; always preparing, but never looking. We secretly wait on God to bless us with a man, but are passively asking for one or not asking at all. Then when the first single (or not) man walks in the door we are all over him. I don't want this to be us anymore. I want us to be comfortable in our waiting and asking of God to bless us. I want us to not be ashamed to say "Yes, I am looking forward to being a wife and I'm going to spend this season preparing AND I'm going to boldly ask God to bless me with my covering (husband)."

I think as single women we've been led to believe that we shouldn't pray boldly for our mate nor should we concern God with it; we should just quietly wait in the corner not praying to be "found." I believe that not only should we ask, but that God cares and is ready to bless us. I also believe we must be ready for the blessing as well. I believe that's what this book does. It prepares us for the blessing ahead and frees us from the chains and bondage of singleness. What sets this book apart is we accomplish this goal by praying for others. We break our own chains by praying God breaks someone else's. We free ourselves by praying for the freedom of others. Helping our sister break free is going to benefit us both. We are not crabs in a bucket pulling each other down nor are we bitter single ladies. We are Daughters of the Most High and we desire to see our sister blessed as much as we want to be blessed.

We can realize that when God blesses her we will be blessed as well.

I'm excited we are taking this journey together. After the 7 days you will have prayed away years of binding chains that have held you and your sister down. God created a whole new world in seven days...I'm believing that in the next 7 days a whole new single you will be created as well.

I love you all from the bottom of my heart. I thank God for crossing our paths. I can't wait to hear the amazing testimonies that will come from the next seven days.

Be Blessed

Nakilah

~Daughter of the Most High~

Acknowledgments

I want to thank God for trusting me with such a humbling mission. I can think of 100 different other women who would have been better suited for the task, but God chose perfectly imperfect me and I'm eternally grateful.

I would also like to thank the two women who were in this with me while the concept was being conceived. This was conceived in our pain and birthed through obedience. Those seven days changed our lives and I'm grateful for the experience.

As always thanks to my family. To my mother; thanks for your insight. Thanks to my children who didn't mind checking me and asking, "Are you working on the book?" As well as, being extra "spicy" about keeping me on task. Thanks to friends, especially Nakia S. who encouraged me along the way. I love you all.

I want to thank my Soul Mate Sister, Marci B, who was pushing the book and concept faster than I could get it on paper. Thank you for sharing with others because you believed in what God was doing. You quickly showed me it wasn't' about me but what God was trying to do in the lives of His daughters.

Last but surely not least. To my brother Larry Gilkey; this is the start of a new chapter in our friendship and I'm still amazed. Who knew over 20 years ago we would be serving in the kingdom together? Amazing how God works. Once I realized we shared the same vision I knew that God was up to something and like I told God, "I definitely want in on this!" This is just the start of something ABSOLUTELY AMAZING! This is the first project of many and you'll never know what you mean to me. I pray God's many blessings on you, your family, your publishing house (which is about to blow up!), and your ministry. Love you much!

Introduction

This book is dedicated to all those women who love God and have faith ten times greater than a mustard seed, but are sick of hearing "There's nothing wrong with you being single." Of course I'm not implying there is anything "wrong" with being single. This is the time when Paul suggests in 2 Corinthians 7:32 that we focus on being about the Lord's work and not distracted with relationships. However, if honest, we can admit that being single is not all it's cracked up to be. After all the work is done: the children have been cared for, we've hit the gym, served in ministry and the day is wrapping up, sometimes we want to curl up in a pair of big strong arms. We want to share our day and listen to his. We want to have conversations where words aren't needed. We want kisses, touches, loving, heck we want to have mind blowing sex and blow his mind in the process. There isn't anything wrong with this, even God approves as long as it's in the boundaries of marriage.

Hearing that we should be happy being single comes from some of the most annoying sources: our married friends, our girlfriend who is wrapped up in a relationship or our bitter friend who is "over men" right now. We're made to believe that we should just do cartwheels because time and time again we are the bridesmaids, but never the bride. We know that King Jesus is all we need, but what about when our bodies "want?" We trust God enough to do it His way. We won't settle for less and we are keeping our "cookies" in the jar. We are smart enough to know that God has the best in store for us. We believe His Word to be true for our lives. We believe we are called to be partners in life with a son of the Most High. We desire to be helpmates, friends, mothers, partners, lovers, prayer warriors and the missing rib for a blessed man. We realize we are the prize and the good thing to be found. This book is not for those who just want a man for sex or because they are lonely. This is for those who realize their union will ultimately bless the Kingdom of God. We're ready for marriage because we've taken the time to work on ourselves, ministries, responsibilities, and we are very much datable and marriage material. If this sounds like you, then you are in the right place for a blessing.

How to use this book

This book is to be shared between two or more friends or a group of women. The women will have:

❖ Someone to pray for

❖ Someone praying for them

Fill out the daily Prayer Cards. One is for your Sister in Prayer and the other is for you. God speaks to us in 3 ways:

1. Through His Word

2. Through the Holy Spirit

3. Through Others

The prayer card for your Sister is for you to share the things God placed on your heart for her. Share your prayer for her as well. Also, the prayer cards are for you to write your own reflections. To write the things you learn about yourself each day as the Holy Spirit reveals it to you.

We ARE NOT to focus on ourselves during this time. If you are in a relationship and desiring God to move it to the next level, then make that known on your prayer card, but you are not to pray for yourself or your own relationship during this time. You will focus solely on your sister in prayer. You will intercede on her behalf for the next seven days. You will fast for her and pray for her and thank God in advance for HER breakthrough. I can hear you now, "But what about me?" This isn't about you…it's beyond you. It's about you being the bridesmaid while you help her become the bride. This is about you exercising your faith and saying "God I trust you enough to take the focus off what I want, and move it to what my sister needs." You are also telling your sister that you trust her enough to pray just as hard for you as you would for yourself, but guess what… she will probably pray even harder because she knows first-hand just how you feel.

This group will grow closer because you are taking your sister's most intimate desires before our Daddy. As you pray for your sister and your sister prays for you, a power will be unleashed in heaven and God will take notice. Matthew 18:20 reminds us that when "two or more are gathered in my name, there am I with them." As two of us come together God will be in the mist and change MUST take place. Singleness will not be all that's prayed away: depression, loneliness, rejection, and low self-esteem, will also be set to flight as you embark on this journey. Remember, if God be for us then nothing else matters!

Agenda for the next Seven Days:

1. Preparation- Joshua 3:5b

2. Motives- Ephesians 5:22-24

3. Submission- James 4:2-3

4. Relationship from Courtship, Ceremony and Beyond- several scriptures

5. Christ-like love- Ephesians 5:25

6. Temptation- Proverbs 5:16, 20 (MSG)

7. Head of the household- Ephesians 5:23

~Day 1~

Preparation

Joshua 3:5b "Consecrate yourselves, for tomorrow the Lord will do amazing things among you."

In order to become someone's life partner, friend, and helpmate, you must be prepared. The prayer focus for the day is Preparation before the relationship. Today you will pray that your sister is ready for marriage. That God prepares her heart, mind, body and spirit to be a wife and partner. The focus scripture is Joshua 3:5. Joshua told the people "Consecrate yourselves, for tomorrow the Lord will do amazing things among you." This was the command given by Joshua when the Children of Israel were preparing to cross the Jordan, win a victory over Jericho and move into The Promised Land. As single women of God, we must do the same thing. We must consecrate ourselves because the Lord is planning to do some amazing things in our lives. Proverbs 31:12 says, "She brings him good, not harm ALL the days of her life." So she needs to be preparing now and honoring her husband now. Jeremiah 29:11 reminds us "For I know the plans I have for you," declares the Lord, "plans to prosper you and not to harm you, plans to give you hope and a future." The man your sister will marry is no surprise to God. It's already done in the spirit and we are just waiting for it to manifest in the natural.

If your sister hasn't made a pledge to God to abstain from sex until marriage, this would be an awesome time to pray for her in this area. Encourage her to take the Purple Bracelet Pledge (see Purple Bracelet Pledge in appendix). You don't want to leave any stone unturned. You must pray that she is setting herself apart so she is prepared to receive her blessing from God. She must operate like she already has the marriage.

Emotions

You should be praying for her to be emotionally stable. She cannot expect to be a wife if she cannot at least make a good attempt to manage her emotions. Of course we all get emotional from time to time, but you want to pray that she is able to operate in wisdom and discernment when it comes to her emotions. Galatians 5:16-17 states "...Live by the Spirit, and you will not gratify the desires of the sinful nature. For the sinful nature desires what is contrary to the Spirit, and the Spirit what is contrary to the sinful nature. They are in conflict with each other, so that

you do not do what you want." You must pray that your
sister is living by the Spirit of God and not living just to
fulfill her sinful nature. You must pray that she learns to
seek God first before she reacts to the ups and downs of
her marriage. As a result, her words and actions will be
pleasing to God and a benefit to her family.

Finances

You should also pray that she is financially prepared,
and if her financial house is not in order that she is
working on it. You must pray that she is a tither, if not,
that she starts and becomes faithful. Proverbs 31 paints a
picture of a woman with her financial house in order. She
works, provides food for her family and she considers
fields and buys them and out of her earnings she plants
vineyards (Proverbs 31:15-18). She is resourceful and has
her own money to take care of business. Pray that your
sister is in the same position or working towards it. Pray

that she can be a financial blessing to her husband and family and not a burden.

Children

Pray for her children if she already has them. Pray they are prepared for a step-father and have a heart to receive him. Also pray for her children's father. Pray he does not cause them any trouble, and that they will have peace in their extended family. Also pray for his children if he has any. Even if you are not sure, pray just in case. Pray they are ready for a step-mother, step-siblings, and extended family. Also pray their mother(s) do not cause any trouble, and that there is peace in their extended family.

Total Preparation

Anything you can think of to pray in order to help her prepare for her mate, PRAY IT! In addition, pray she is a good housekeeper, if not; pray she is working on it. If she's not a good cook or doesn't like to be "domesticated" (cook, clean, take care of home), pray she works on this area as well. Men like to eat in a clean house, so pray she can provide this environment for her husband. Pray she's prepared to satisfy his needs sexually. Marriage is not the time to practice being a prude. It is the time to let your hair down and be your husband's fantasy! Hebrews 13:4 (KJV) reminds us that marriage is honorable in all and that the bed is undefiled. Also, 1 Corinthians 7:4-5 reminds us that our bodies are not our own and not to deprive each other of sex unless it is mutual and for an agreed upon amount of time; for times of fasting and praying. Pray your sister and her husband have a healthy, happy, and active life. Anything else you can think to pray to help her prepare for her marriage, PRAY IT!

Prayer Starter

Heavenly Father today I pray for my sister. I pray that you prepare her heart, mind, body, and soul for the call and mission of marriage. Touch every aspect of her life and begin to prepare her to be all that she can be for her husband. Prepare her for the role of helpmate as you have called us to be in Genesis 2:18. She has consecrated herself today believing that you are about to do something amazing in her life…

<u>Daily Prayer Card Day 1</u>

For Your Sister in Prayer:

<u>*Daily Prayer Card Day 1*</u>

For You:

✓ **How can I be better prepared for marriage?**

~Day 2~

Motives

James 4:2b-3 " You do not have because you do not ask God when you ask you do not receive, because you ask with wrong motives, that you may spend what you get on your pleasures."

Yesterday you prayed for your sister to go through the preparation process for marriage. Today you will focus on her motives. When I say motives, I mean why she wants to get married. Getting married is more than just combatting loneliness or because everyone else is getting married.

There has to be a desire far beyond the physical. How will our marriage be a blessing to others? Will we be a blessing to our spouse or do we just want our needs met? Are we willing and ready to put our own desires aside in order to please our partner? We must go beyond wanting someone to take to the family reunion; but someone we want to assist in ministry, to be a helpmate to. We have to be ready to give up what we want for what our partner needs.

So you must focus on praying that your sister's motives line up with the Lord's will. Jesus said in Matthew 7:7 that "if we ask it will be given to us" but here in the focus scripture for the day, James 4:2b-3, we're being reminded that we didn't have the things we wanted either because we didn't ask for it, or because we asked with the wrong motives. You want to make sure your sister is prepared and her motives line up with God's will for marriage. We are all aware of what we want to get from our partner; love, affection, sex, intimacy, partnership, but what are we willing to give? How do our motives bless the kingdom (will others be blessed by our union)? There are so many things that we have to consider when desiring marriage. When our motives line up right we can ask and shall receive. Since you are the one praying for her and her marriage, then the motives won't be selfish and will be generously given from the heart.

Prayer Starter

Heavenly Father I give you the glory and honor. I magnify you. Lord I pray for my sister's motives for marriage. I pray her union will not just bless her, but her husband and those around them as well. I pray she is able to put her needs aside having full trust that you will take care of them, and seek to satisfy the needs of the one she will marry. Help her to have a heart to serve and that her intentions are set on your will. I don't want her to not have

because her intentions are not properly lined up.

Daily Prayer Card Day 2

For Your Sister in Prayer:

Daily Prayer Card Day 2

For You:

✓ **What is motivating me to get married?**

✓ **What is my REAL WHY?**

~Day 3~

Submission

Wives, submit yourselves to your own husbands as you do to the Lord. "For the husband is the head of the wife as Christ is the head of the church, his body, of which he is the savior. Now as the church submits to Christ, so also wives should submit to their husbands in everything." Ephesians 5:22-24

Today is all about submission. I know, I know! It's like a bad word in women's circles, but if God commands it then it must be designed to bless us. Let's look at the concept of submission. One of the dictionary's definitions of the word submit is to "give over or yield to the power or authority of another." We are often afraid that if we submit to someone we lose power over our lives, but if we trust God and do it His way, we gain far more than we give up. Following God's Word and the direction of the Holy Spirit will lead us in the right direction and will allow us to come under a man who is following God. We can trust the man that God blesses us with. Ephesians 5:22-24 says that we must submit to our husbands as to the Lord, what it doesn't say is women submit to a man because he's a man. We have to be willing and ready to submit to our HUSBAND, but use wisdom and discernment when doing so. Meaning, when we are seriously dating a man and moving towards marriage we have to show that we can and are willing to follow but not give full husband privileges. Let him take the lead as the Lord lays it on his heart.

Now that you realize submitting to our husband is not just a good idea but it pleases God, you should be eager and excited to pray for your sister to have a heart of submission for her husband. If she desires for him to love her like Christ loves the church, then she must be willing to submit to him like the Church submits to Christ. Pray that she can follow his lead and assist him in making decision for the family. She needs to be able to trust his decision; therefore, pray that he is following God so she can properly follow him.

Also pray that during your sister's time of singleness she is sharpening the skill of submission by submitting to the Lord. Pray that she is listening to the voice of the Holy Spirit daily, and submitting to the will of the Lord. She will already have a heart to submit to her husband in marriage if she is submitting to the Lord in her singleness.

Prayer Starter

Dear Lord, Thank you for your word and for your order. Thank you that you operate in order and never in chaos. Lord today I pray that you give our sister the heart of submission, and that she has a desire to follow her husband. Lord our society celebrates the thought of women not following their husband, but I realize we are not to conform to the ways of this world but to live by your Word. We come against that spirit right now in Jesus name. We thank you for our equal rights, but we bless and honor the order you have set in your plan. I pray that my sister embraces her place and humbly submits herself to her husband as the church submits itself to Christ.

Submission

Daily Prayer Card Day 3

For Your Sister in Prayer:

Daily Prayer Card Day 3

For You:

✓ **Am I truly ready for submission that is pleasing to God?**

✓ **How can I better submit to God?**

~Day 4~

Relationship

Day four brings us halfway through this awesome process. So this day will be dedicated to praying for the relationship as a whole. You will be praying for their whole relationship: from the courtship, to the ceremony, and onto the conclusion of their relationship when death does them apart. This is also a day you will fast for your sister and her relationship. You want God to know just how serious you are about your sister being found. It doesn't matter how you choose to fast, just sacrifice for your sister. Praying and fasting unselfishly is pleasing to God. Giving of ourselves for our neighbor is God's desire and command. "This is the kind of fast day I'm {God} after: to break the chains of injustice, get rid of exploitation in the workplace, free the oppressed, cancel debts. What I'm interested in seeing you do is: sharing your food with the hungry, inviting the homeless poor into your homes, putting clothes on the shivering ill-clad, being available to your own families. Do this and the lights will turn on, and your lives will turn around at once. Your righteousness will pave your way. The God of glory will secure your passage. Then when you pray, God will answer. You'll call out for help and I'll say, 'Here I am.' (Isaiah 58:6-9 MSG)."Hebrews 13:16 reminds us to "do not forget to do good and to share with others, for with such sacrifices God is pleased." God will see your heart and the desire you have for your sister to be blessed and He will honor that. Take this day to pray for everything! Pray for their first encounter if your prayer partner is not currently seeing anyone, and pray for their courtship. Pray that God helps them stay on the right path. Pray that their engagement is everything they imagine it to be. Pray the wedding ceremony goes well. Pray their honeymoon is utterly amazing! Pray for them to have good communication, good sex, financial security, and that they achieve their goals; and pray against adultery. Pray their family is blessed, and if they are a blended family, pray that it goes as God plans. Pray God will ALWAYS be the head.

This is also a good time to take a praise break for your sister. Thank God for what she is about to receive. James1:6 remind us that when we ask, we must believe and not doubt. So thank God with expectancy! You are going boldly before the throne laying your petitions down before the Lord for your sister, so you should expect God not to just HEAR us, but to ANSWER us as well. Psalm 116:1

declares "I love the Lord, for he heard my voice; he heard my cry for mercy. Psalm 21:2 encourages us by saying "You have granted him (her) his heart's desire and have not withheld the request of his (her) lips." Psalm 118:21 declares that "I will give you thanks, for you answered me. You have become my salvation." So throw a praise party celebrating what your sister is about to receive. Thank the Lord for hearing your earnest plea for her.

Scriptures for Day 4

- Hosea 2:19 (being married to God)

- Genesis 1:27-28 (God's command to Adam and Eve)

- Genesis 2:21-25 (creation of Eve and their union)

- Malachi 2:14-15 (being unfaithful)

- 1 Corinthians 7:2 (having sex with your own husband or wife)

- Hebrews 13:4 (marriage being honored, and the bed being pure)

- Galatians 5:22-23 (fruits of the Spirit)

- Exodus 20:14 and Proverbs 6:23 (both deal with adultery)

Prayer Starter

Awesome and wonderful Lord, I come to you with a praise on my lips and a song in my heart, giving you the glory and praise. Thank you for what my sister is about to receive! Thank you in advance for blessing her with a wonderful son whom you saw fit to choose. Lord I pray that you bless their relationship from the first encounter until one goes home to glory. I pray their courtship is blessed. I pray that you put a hedge of protection around them to keep the enemy away. Let your Word drown out the advice of the world. Let them follow your plan and design for a relationship and ignore what society says it should be. Allow them to be on your time table and not the world's. Let them know quickly that this is the relationship chosen for them and let them find peace in it. Lord I pray they look past the ceremony and "getting married" and focus on staying married. Bless every aspect of their relationship from faith to finances and family. Let them find peace, love, and joy in each other because their relationship lies in You. Be with them and guide them through good times and bad. Through all that life has to offer and all that you have planned.

~Intermission~

You are halfway through this process of praying the single away. You have spent the first three days focused on your sister: that she is prepared for marriage; has the correct motives for marriage, and her obedience in the area of submission in marriage. Day four was spent on the relationship as a whole from start to finish. Therefore you will spend the last three days focusing on her husband. I don't consider him to be her future husband because I truly believe God has already worked the whole thing out, and all we're waiting for is a manifestation in the natural (Jeremiah 39:11). This is why it is important to operate in certain ways now because we are bringing our husbands honor all the days of our life and that means NOW (Proverbs 31:12)!

<u>Daily Prayer Card Day 4</u>

For Your Sister in Prayer:

<u>Daily Prayer Card Day 4</u>

For You:

~Day 5~

Christ-like Love

Husbands, love your wives, just as Christ loved the church and gave himself up for her to make her holy, cleansing her by the washing with water through the word, and to present her to himself as a radiant church, without stain or wrinkle or any other blemish, but holy and blameless. In this same way, husbands ought to love their wives as their own bodies. He who loves his wife loves himself. After all, no one ever hated their own body, but they feed and care for their

body, just as Christ does the church" Ephesians 5:25-29

Today you are praying that your sister's husband loves her like Christ loves the church. We hear this scripture so often, but do we really understand what it means. In order to have a clear understanding we have to first understand what Christ's love for the church looks like. The Message translation of Ephesians 5:25-29 paints a really good picture:

> Husbands, go all out in your love for your wives, exactly as Christ did for the church—a love marked by giving, not getting. Christ's love makes the church whole. His words evoke her beauty. Everything he does and says is designed to bring the best out of her, dressing her in dazzling white silk, radiant with holiness. And that is how husbands ought to love their

wives. They're really doing themselves a favor—since they're already "one" in marriage.

So you are asking God to help her husband realize that "Everything he does and says is designed to bring the best out of her." You are praying that he realizes he must be dedicated to loving, caring for, and uplifting her. As a result, he is in essence loving, caring, and uplifting himself. Furthermore, he is really doing himself a favor since they are one in marriage.

Prayer Starter

Heavenly Father, today I lift up my sister's husband. I pray he loves her like Christ loves the church. I pray he realizes when he lifts her up; he lifts up himself as well. We pray he goes all out in his love for her like Christ does for us. We pray everything he does and says is to bring out the best in her. Help him to understand how You love us Lord, so he can love her in a way that is pleasing to You and edifying to her.

<u>*Daily Prayer Card Day 5*</u>

For Your Sister in Prayer:

Daily Prayer Card Day 5

For You:

✓ **How can you display Christ-like love to your mate and to others?**

~Day 6~

Temptation

"Do you know the saying, "Drink from your own rain barrel, draw water from your own spring-fed well"? It's true. Otherwise, one day you may come home and find your barrel empty and your well polluted. "Your spring water is for you and you only, not to be passed around among strangers. Bless your fresh-flowing fountain! Enjoy the wife you married as a young man! Lovely as an angel, beautiful as a rose—don't ever quit taking delight in her body. Never take

her love for granted! Why would you trade enduring intimacies for cheap thrills with a whore? for dalliance with a promiscuous stranger?" Proverbs 5:16, 20 MSG

Today is very important. According to statistics, 50-60 percent of marriages in the US are affected by adultery. Temptation is **EVERYWHERE.** Even men with the best intentions will be faced with temptation. In Matthew 4 Jesus was tempted by the devil. He had been fasting, was hungry and the first thing the enemy offered was something to eat and that's just how it is in the world. Some of our sisters and even us, have sent our husbands/men out into the world hungry and please believe the enemy is waiting with a big old plate of what he needs and wants. Today, you want to pray that not only can your sister's husband resist temptation; but that her goal and mission is to make sure he never leaves home hungry. You want to pray your sister's husband is able to withstand the temptations of this world. The book of Proverbs is filled with warnings of the adulterous woman. Your focus scripture today encourages couples to enjoy the pleasures of their own marriage. The reference to the well and water relates to how important the well and water was to families, likewise our partners should be important to us as well. As you pray today, pray that your sister's husband is operating in wisdom and discernment. Pray he is covered and filled with the Holy Spirit and able to withstand the fiery arrows of the enemy. Also pray for their sex life. Pray it's pleasing and satisfying. Pray God blesses their intimate union and they have pleasure until death do them part.

Prayer Starter

Heavenly Father, today I pray that my sister's husband is able to resist temptation. I pray that he finds pleasure in my sister all the days of his life. I pray that she does her part in making sure her husband is satisfied. I pray that he resists the tricks of the enemy and is able to remain faithful to my sister. I pray that she satisfies him always and that he will forever be captivated by her love. I pray their sex life is full of pleasure, fun, excitement, variety with one another and they find satisfaction in You and each other all the days of their life.

<u>Daily Prayer Card Day 6</u>

For Your Sister in Prayer:

Daily Prayer Card Day 6

For You:

✓ **How can you help fight against temptation?**

~Day 7~

Head of the Household

For the husband is the head of the wife as Christ is the head of the church, his body, of which he is the Savior. Ephesians 5:23

Today is the final day of praying for your sister and her husband. Today you will be focusing on praying that her husband will fall into his place as head of the household. Ephesians states that as "Christ is the head of the church the husband is the head of his household." Many of our brothers have a hard time stepping into this role. Either they don't know what their role is or there is a power struggle to fulfill it. On day three you prayed that your sister is submissive to him, and that if she respects God's order for marriage, then the only issue will be her husband knowing his role. It's a common misconception that this means he is dominate or that the wife's opinion doesn't matter, but that is not true. It is all about God's order. God desires for the husband to be the head over his family. During biblical times, the man of the house was the lord and priest of his home, and his family was submitted under him, with the idea that he is submitted under God. The decisions of the man determined the fate of the whole family. It wasn't until Adam ate the fruit that the fate of the world changed. An example of a whole family being blessed through the father is Noah. Genesis 7:1 "The Lord then said to Noah, "Go into the ark, you and your whole family, because I have found you righteous in this generation..

The story of Achan is an example of when a man sins against God and his whole family suffers from his decision. Joshua 7:24-25"Then Joshua, together with all Israel, took Achan son of Zerah, the silver, the robe, the gold bar, his sons and daughters, his cattle, donkeys and sheep, his tent and all that he had, to the Valley of Achor. 25 Joshua said, "Why have you brought this trouble on us? The Lord will bring trouble on you today." Then all Israel stoned him, and after they had stoned the rest, they burned them."

This is why today's prayer is important. Not only are you praying that he steps up in this role, but that he is successful in it. The family's fate rests in him being the head of his household.

Prayer Starter

Father today we pray for your sister's husband. I pray that you bless him in his role as head of the household. I pray that he realizes the importance of this role and how his decisions affect the whole family. I pray my sister falls into her role and her husband values her opinion; that they work as a partnership, but at the end of the day she realizes he is the head and has the last say.

Last Day! Praise Break!

For the past seven days you have prayed for your sister and her marriage. You have covered her and her husband in prayer. You have taken these seven days to put aside your own needs, emotions, desires and wants in order to put her requests before the Father. By now you should have prayed away your own singleness. You should have realized that it wasn't all about you and that you have a higher call to intercede on the behalf of others. You have gone to the Father in confidence for someone else! There are several lessons that you should have learned during this time. Compare the prayer cards your sister in prayer gave you with the notes you recorded each day for yourself. Did

God reveal things to you and they were confirmed through your sister in prayer? What did you learn about yourself during this time? How can you grow to be who God is calling you to be? There are also a few other lessons you should have gleaned during this time as well:

- ❖ You have pleased God by unselfishly praying for someone else, their future, and THEIR HAPPINESS.

- ❖ You should have realized that you are not alone

- ❖ You should feel better about knowing that you have prayed for someone else and someone else has prayed for you.

No longer can the enemy use your singleness against you because you realize God has your husband on the way, and being single is just a season you are currently in. The task of praying for someone else should have also helped you realize God can use you during this season and how important the SINGLE you is to the Kingdom of God.

Spend some time with the sister you prayed for. Continue to encourage her past these seven days. You have prayed for the most intimate details of her future and her marriage and you should continue to keep her in your prayers. When YOU begin to feel down or discouraged by your own singleness, take some time to pray for her or another single sister. Repeat this prayer circle often to keep the enemy at bay, your spirit encouraged, and your sister and her husband lifted in prayer. Spend time reviewing your prayer cards and begin to ask God to help you in those areas. Seek out ways to continue to serve God and encourage other women. Be open to be used by God. Get busy working in the field… Boaz never would have seen Ruth if she wasn't in the field working (Ruth 2). Singleness is a season not to be ruled by loneliness, but by your desire to serve God with your whole heart and allow Him to use you beyond you. Be Strong, Be Single, Be a Servant for God. Charm is deceptive, and beauty is fleeting; but a woman who fears the Lord is to be praised (Proverbs 31:30).

Daughter of the Most High Affirmation

I am a Daughter of the Most High. I am fearfully and wonderfully made. I am beautiful, whole, and complete. Everything I need can be found in and provided by my Father. I don't have to beg for anything or anyone's attention. I realize that I am the prize, the good thing to be found. I will not beg for scraps when I know that my Father has prepared a table for me. I am empowered, encouraged, educated and edified. God has opened my eyes to see that I can do all and be all I've been called to be through Christ who strengthens me. I will allow the Holy Spirit to guide and direct me as I begin again the kingdom way and receive all that my Father has for me. I am beautiful and whole and perfectly me. I am a Daughter of the Most High, just who I've been called to be.

Daily Prayer Card Day 7

For Your Sister in Prayer:

Daily Prayer Card Day 7

For You:

✓ **How can what you learned about submission help your husband be successful at running the household?**

Appendix

The Purple Bracelet

The Purple Bracelet is a bracelet we wear to signify our desire to wait on our husband for sex. It is a bracelet that says "Daughter of the Most High" on one side and "Saving it for Daddy" on the other. It is simply a vow to wait until the time is right for sex. Sex often causes many issues within our relationships when we jump into it too soon. As women, we get emotionally involved and fail to make good choices when sex becomes a part of our relationships. While taking the Purple Bracelet pledge, we vow to respect God, our self, and our future. It causes us to think twice about giving our bodies to a man who is not our husband let alone our committed partner. During this time of prayer, pray about your sister taking this pledge. Pray that she considers saving her body for "The One." If you haven't made this commitment, pray about making it as well.